# All about
# BUS DRIVERS

**Brianna Kaiser**

Lerner Publications ◆ Minneapolis

## Who Are the People in Your Neighborhood?

*Sesame Street* has always been set smack in the middle of a friendly, busy community. We know that for all children, getting to know their communities is crucially important. So is understanding that everyone in that neighborhood—including kids!—has a part to play. In the *Sesame Street®️ Loves Community Helpers* books, *Sesame Street*'s favorite furry friends help young readers get to know some of these helpers better.

Sincerely,
The Editors at Sesame Workshop

# Table of Contents

We Love Bus Drivers!                4

Learn about Bus Drivers            6

Thank You, Bus Drivers!            28
Picture Glossary                        30
Read More                                31
Index                                        31

# We Love Bus Drivers!

Bus drivers are fantastic! They take me to school and back home.

# Learn about Bus Drivers

Bus drivers are community helpers. They bring passengers where they need to go.

My mom and I take the bus to the park.

Some bus drivers drive school buses.

School buses are big and yellow, like me.

They take students to school and back home.

# Some bus drivers drive city buses.

Elmo's family rides the bus to the museum.

They drive people to work and other places in the city.

Bus drivers make sure people get on and off the bus safely.

Bus drivers are helpful.

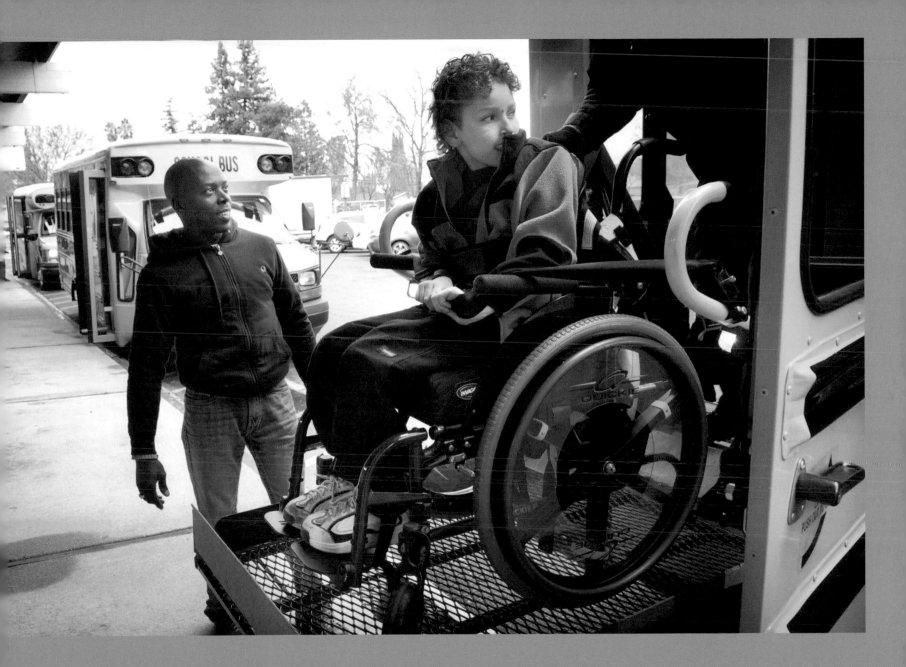

They use a lift for people who use wheelchairs.

**Bus drivers are good drivers. They keep their eyes on the road.**

Bus drivers make sure people get to places safely.

You can help your bus driver by staying in your seat and talking quietly.

It's fun to ride the school bus with my friend Elmo.

You can also help your bus driver by making sure the aisle is clear.

I put my backpack in my lap to keep the aisle clear.

All bus drivers learn routes. Then they know where to pick up passengers.

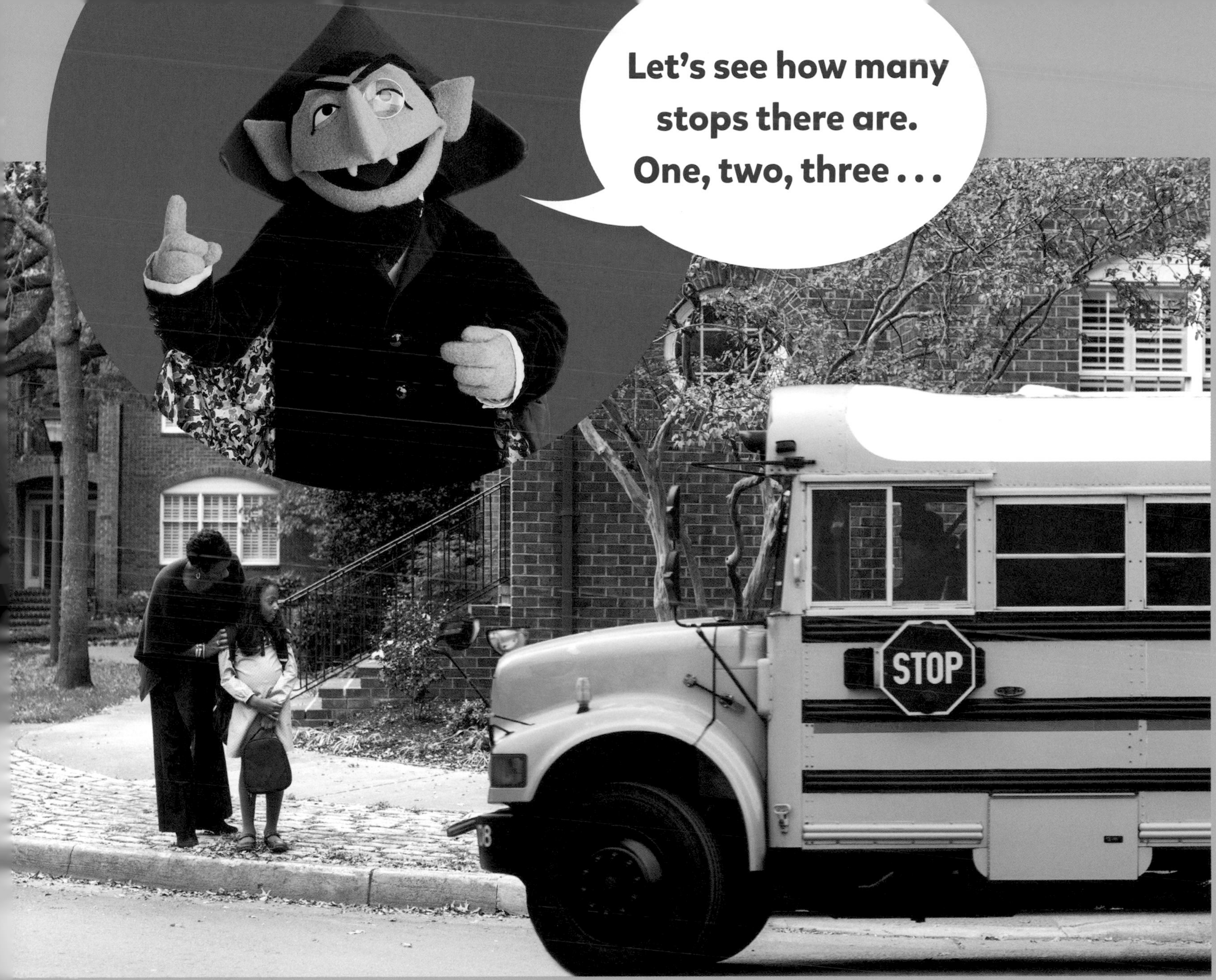
Let's see how many stops there are. One, two, three . . .
STOP

They also follow a schedule. Schedules tell them when to pick up and drop off passengers.

I get on my bus at eight in the morning.

They drive in rain, snow, and sunshine.

Ernie and I take the bus when it's raining so we don't get wet.

**Bus drivers work hard. They are always ready to help people.**

Now it's your turn! Write a thank-you note to your favorite bus driver.

Dear Bus Driver,

Thank you for getting me to places safely. I love taking the bus!

Your friend,

Rosita

# Picture Glossary

**community:** a place where people live and work

**passengers:** people riding on the bus

**routes:** the paths a bus takes

**schedule:** a list of times that a bus stops and goes places

## Read More

Honders, Christine. *Bus Drivers*. New York: PowerKids, 2020.

Mattern, Joanne. *We Go on a School Bus*. Egremont, MA: Red Chair, 2020.

Reinke, Beth Bence. *School Buses on the Go*. Minneapolis: Lerner Publications, 2018.

## Index

aisle, 18

passengers, 6, 20, 22

routes, 20

schedule, 22

school, 4, 8–9

## Photo Acknowledgments

Image credits: sirtravelalot/Shutterstock.com, p. 5; SDI Productions/E+/Getty Images, pp. 6, 19, 22, 30 (passenger) (schedule); David Grossman/Alamy Stock Photo, pp. 7, 30 (community); martinedoucet/E+/Getty Images, p. 8; MBPROJEKT_Maciej_Bledowski/iStock/Getty Images, p. 9; Edward Westmacott/Alamy Stock Photo, p. 10; ollo/iStock/Getty Images, p. 11; Syda Productions/Shutterstock.com, p. 12; ZUMA Press Inc/Alamy Stock Photo, pp. 13, 26; Vladimir Vladimirov/E+/Getty Images, p. 14; MikeDotta/Shutterstock.com, p. 15; Brand X Pictures/Stockbyte/Getty Images, p. 16; kali9/iStock/Getty Images, p. 17; SolStock/E+/Getty Images, p. 18; wdstock/iStock/Getty Images, pp. 20, 30 (route); Roberto Westbrook/Getty Images, p. 21; moodboard/Getty Images, p. 23; fotog/Getty Images, p. 24; kali9/E+/Getty Images, p. 27; Africa Studio/Shutterstock.com, p. 29.

Cover: LightField Studios/Shutterstock.com.

Lerner Publications Company
An imprint of Lerner Publishing Group, Inc.
241 First Avenue North
Minneapolis, MN 55401 USA

For reading levels and more information, look up this title at www.lernerbooks.com.

Main body text set in Mikado Medium.
Typeface provided by HVD Fonts.

**Designer:** Mary Ross
**Lerner team:** Martha Kranes

**Library of Congress Cataloging-in-Publication Data**

Names: Kaiser, Brianna, 1996- author.
Title: All about bus drivers / Brianna Kaiser.
Description: Minneapolis : Lerner Publications , 2023. | Series: Sesame Street loves community helpers | Includes bibliographical references and index. | Audience: Ages 4–8 | Audience: Grades K–1 | Summary: "Communities rely on bus drivers. They safely get people where they need to go. Join the furry friends from Sesame Street to learn more about these helpers" — Provided by publisher.
Identifiers: LCCN 2021040285 (print) | LCCN 2021040286 (ebook) | ISBN 9781728456140 (library binding) | ISBN 9781728462103 (ebook)
Subjects: LCSH: Bus drivers—Juvenile literature.
Classification: LCC HD8039.M8 K35 2022  (print) | LCC HD8039.M8  (ebook) | DDC 388.3/22—dc23/eng/20211015

LC record available at https://lccn.loc.gov/2021040285
LC ebook record available at https://lccn.loc.gov/2021040286

Manufactured in the United States of America
1-50684-50103-1/25/2022